how To Live in fLip-fLops

sandy gingras

SOURCEBOOKS, INC.®
NAPERVILLE, ILLINOIS

Published by Sourcebooks, Inc.
P.O. Box 4410, Naperville, Illinois 60567-4410
(630) 961-3900
Fax: (630) 961-2168
www.sourcebooks.com

Printed and bound in China.
OGP 10 9 8 7 6 5 4 3 2 1

"Always maintain a kind of summer, even in the middle of winter."

Henry David Thoreau

how To Live
in flip-flops

A life in flip-flops is a cheery life (it's hard to take ourselves seriously when our shoes are making funny noises). It's a slow life (difficult to run in such flappy shoes). It's easy (slide in-slide out) and sunny (wear SPF on every toe). It's a life as casual and silly and colorful and sweet as the designs upon our feet...

When we open up our feet to the sun, our lives seem to open up also — to the stars and the moon, to the sky, to the possibilities of the horizon.

Perhaps the equation: free toes =
free self seems too simple. But when a
woman changes her wardrobe, she
changes her mood, her mind, and

maybe
even
her
life
too.

(before)   (after)

Think of Cinderella absolutely
transformed by her shoes...

Flip-flops are as much attitude as they are footwear. They are a verb as much as they are a noun:

flip-flop\'flip-fläp\v. to suddenly reverse direction or point of view

gone to the beach forever →

I have a pair of faded green flip-flops that are soft corduroy with cork soles and, sometimes, when I slip them on, I'm a kid again. I'm transported away from my adult self, and I'm seven years old heading off to the beach with my towel and raft as if that's all I'll ever need in life. I'm transformed into my flip-flop self, distilled down to my simple carefree essence. I'm dreamy and free and radiantly alive.

We all have
moments like this
when we become
the flip-flop
opposite of our
usual selves...

We reverse our point of view.

today's
wardrobe
choices

We lighten up and
uncomplicate.

we

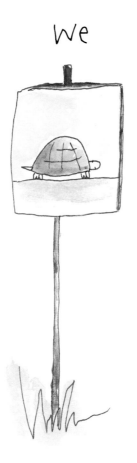

downshift.

And we arrive at a state of mind that's altogether magical in its simplicity.

It's not a faraway exotic locale
(although that would be nice too...).
It's just a moment we inhabit in
an exotic way — a choice we make
to live more playfully, to live more
alive...

to build the castle
(not just watch)
and then to JUMP ALL OVER IT...

to laugh out loud
and
wiggle our toes

to let our
hearts
fly

to dance in the sun.

It doesn't take magic to get us to our flip-flop selves,

it
takes

(and perhaps some sticky
note reminders...).

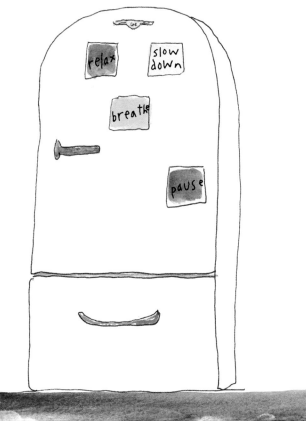

Our to-do lists are so big, they've taken over our lives,

Somehow, we've convinced ourselves that taking any time for us is... well... selfish...

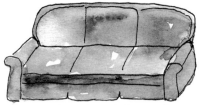

The SELFish couch
(not to be sat upon)

(not to be indulged in)

(not to be lit just for us).

The SELfish candle

Come out and play...

just for a
moment...

Because everyone has the time
and energy in our lives for a moment...

to be ourselves...

not  to do ...

because we've done enough
      for the moment.

  we have enough
       for the moment.

  We are enough
        for the moment.

  Just BE in

The MOMENT

and
wondrously
strange...

We are never as far away
from our flip-flop selves as
we might feel.

If we just give
ourselves a moment,
we can

open up

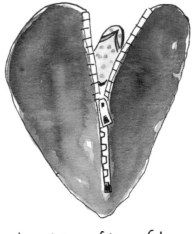

to the flip-flop
self within;

The
philosophy
of
the flip-
flop...

I hope you find your flip-flop self...
the happy sound of your own walk,
a soft-easy on a hard path,
a kind of snap-crackle-pop of your childhood,
a silly yet sublime beat of aliveness

as you make your way ahead...

I hope your flip-flop days
are full of moments...

like a sky whirled with
stars,
like a table glowing with
candles,
and a garden full of
daisies...

like a beach full
of sunshine.

I hope you pause and soak
in these moments.

I hope you savor
the small sweet things.

I hope you...

get the beach chair with the most settings for recline

smell like a coconut

siesta and siesta and siesta...

take a

Long deep breath.

trust your dreams.

I hope you know that if you stay between the channel markers all the time, you'll never find your own path.

And when a new
day opens,
I hope you open
your door,
open your heart,
and go out
and play in it...
Live
in your flip-flops...

Since she was a little girl, Sandy Gingras has been doodling and writing stories, trying to figure out life's mysteries (her hero is still Nancy Drew). She lives in a happy cottage on the bay on an island in New Jersey with her almost-grown-up son and a wonderful golden retriever and two ridiculous cats. You can read more about Sandy and what she does at www.how-to-live.com.

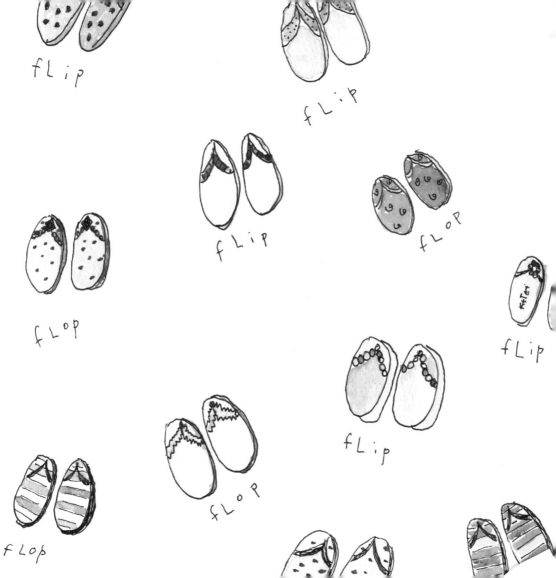

fLip

fLip

fLip

fLop

fLop

fLop

fLip

fLip

fLop